# OFFICIAL GUIDEBOOK

By Kiel Phegley

Scholastic Inc.

Published by Scholastic Inc., *Publishers since 1920*. SCHOLASTIC and associated logos are trademarks and/or registered trademarks of Scholastic Inc.

10 9 8 7 6 5 4 3 2 1     17 18 19 20 21

ISBN 978-1-338-20231-1

Printed in the U.S.A. 40

First printing 2017

Imagine a sporting event where the roar of the crowd is matched by the thunderous sounds on the track. Imagine a sport where competitors spin, smash, flip, and fly their way to glory. Imagine an event unlike any other, entertaining millions of fans on five continents.

Well, you don't have to imagine. This is MONSTER JAM!

The pinnacle of automotive technology, daring stunts, and major speed, Monster Jam trucks deliver in-your-face action across the globe. These 12,000-pound vehicles tower over other trucks on imposing sixty-six-inch tires. And their work-of-art truck bodies growl to life with custom flames, teeth, spikes, and even creatures from beyond.

This book provides you with your very own glimpse inside the world of Monster Jam. From the most famous legends of the track to the tips and tricks that can make you a world-class Monster Jam athlete, it's all here. Get ready to rip it and roll!

# Contents

## Monster Jam: The Big Show

## Monster Jam Achieves the Impossible

## Pit Party

**Welcome to... MONSTER JAM UNIVERSITY**

**W**hat does it take to turn the best of the best in motor sports into a Monster Jam superstar? An education at Monster Jam University!

Located in Paxton, Illinois, at the home of eleven-time World Champion athlete Tom Meents, this university is unlike any classroom you've ever seen. It's the premier testing ground for high-flying jumps, wicked new wheelies, and other never-before-seen stunts. At MJU, "Professor" Meents runs new athletes through the tough physical conditioning they need to operate Monster Jam trucks as well as superfast ATVs and Speedsters.

In the pages ahead, you can train up on what makes Monster Jam trucks come alive. Master the specs of their supercharged engines, get driving tips from the masters as you learn the rules behind major competitions, and prepare to put your pedal to the metal in the Monster Jam arena.

# The BODY

**T**he custom-painted fiberglass bodies of Monster Jam trucks don't just display the wild personalities at the heart of the sport. They also house the high-tech gear that allows athletes to push it to the limit. And with radical "bolt-ons" adding teeth, tongues, tails, and more, these vehicles are almost more monster than machine.

## The Skeleton

Called the roll cage, the core of the truck's chassis is a solid steel structure that keeps the athlete safe. In Monster Jam, these cages are often as colorful as the detailed airbrushed bodies that give each ride its radical persona.

## Big Wheels

In order to tackle dirt tracks, the tires of Monster Jam trucks have to be big and bad— some sixty-six inches tall and forty-three inches wide! Designed and custom-made for Monster Jam by BKT tires, these massive wheels do more than bounce around. The deep treads of the tires give the tire extra "bite" into the dirt so Monster Jam trucks can grip and grind better than any vehicle in the world.

# of the Beast

## The Chair in the Air

Sitting in the seat of a Monster Jam truck is like riding high on a wild animal. But this ride is much safer thanks to custom-molded seats fitted to each individual athlete. Add on a five-point harness to hold the athlete steady, and the seat holds strong through even the gnarliest tricks.

## Super Shocks

How does a Monster Jam truck survive the earth-shaking impact of its many jumps? Thanks to a super suspension system! These behemoths are built on a four-link suspension that keeps the front and back halves separate and flexible. But the most important components are the massive coil-over shocks: These nitrogen-charged shocks help a Monster Jam truck bounce back from the most punishing landings.

## SCIENCE JAM

Did you know that Monster Jam truck tires are so large and sturdy it only takes twenty-three pounds of air pressure to fill them up? (Normal car tires need around thirty pounds of pressure!) These giant tires weigh eight hundred to nine hundred pounds each!

# What Makes a Monster Truck GO!

**N**othing about a Monster Jam truck is average, and the engine is no exception! Sitting on the back of the truck chassis, these vicious, vrooming motors bring Monster Jam to life with an unparalleled 1,500-horsepower output and more noise than an ear-splitting thunderstorm.

## Get Blown Away

To help them heft their heavy bodies high in the air, Monster Jam truck engines are supercharged. That's done with heavy-duty "blower motors," which force a combination of air and fuel into the engine to juice up its horsepower.

## Burning Bright

Unlike standard trucks, Monster Jam trucks run on methanol, an alcohol-based fuel. In order to run a course, Monster Jam competitors will burn through two and a half gallons of methanol in only two minutes! To ensure safety, this powerful mixture is held in a specially designed fuel cell that's puncture-resistant.

## Safe & Secure

Many features are built into the engines of Monster Jam trucks to keep the athletes safe. For example, in competition the officials can trigger a Remote Ignition Interrupter (a handheld radio device) to shut down the truck if needed, and every Monster Jam truck is equipped with a safety pin called the cutoff switch that can completely turn the truck off in an emergency. In addition to these cutting-edge technologies, every athlete has a personal fire extinguisher on hand in the cab to keep themselves safe.

# TIPS
## for the Track

**B**efore you can take a Monster Jam truck for a spin, be sure to study up on the ins and outs of steering these monsters through the course.

## Need for Speed

Whether rolling up a hill or jumping off a ramp, Monster Jam athletes always want to avoid a "nose plant" where the truck lands face-first in the dirt. The way to do this is to pour on the speed. Athletes always say you have to keep pressure on the throttle even after you've launched off the ground. Your tires need to keep moving in the air. As they say on the track, "When in doubt, throttle out."

## Steering Clear

One of the secrets of Monster Jam trucks is that they have separate steering controls for both the front and rear axles. That means you control the front tires with the steering wheel while steering for the rear tires is controlled by a switch that operates an electric pump. It gets tricky, but it makes doing donuts much easier!

## Getting Big Air

Monster Jam trucks are known for jumping over obstacles as big as school buses and for popping straight vertical leaps into the air. But no matter how big the jump, the secret to wowing fans is timing. Athletes need the right size ramp and to hit the throttle at the perfect moment going over the top of it. As always, practice makes perfect.

## Safety First

Any veteran Monster Jam athlete will tell you that good driving starts with proper safety gear, including an essential super-tough helmet made of fiberglass and Kevlar. Similarly, an athlete's racing suit, gloves, and safety shoes are made of fire-resistant material.

# The Field of
# PLAY

**M**onster Jam tracks have evolved far beyond the muddy pits of the past. Today, constructing a competition field is almost as massive a job as building a truck!

Since many Monster Jam competitions are held at sporting arenas, the first step in preparing for the event is covering up the grass or concrete of the host arena without damaging it. Up to 100,000 square feet of plastic and 6,000 sheets of plywood are used to cover the field.

The next step involves bringing in the obstacles for a Monster Jam event, including piles of cars to be crushed by massive Monster Jam tires, dumpsters to serve as safety barriers, and other ramps and jumps.

Once in place, the crew will cart 7,500 tons of dirt onto the field to pack down the track that Monster Jam trucks will go wild on.

Finally, the track needs to be decorated both for the events and for the major Pit Parties thrown for fans. This requires thirty gallons of paint and 1,200 feet of banners. Then officials and athletes both will "eyeball the track" to see what action lies ahead for the evening.

# Rules of the RACE

**W**hile Monster Jam trucks are all about style, speed rules in the racing competition. At any official Monster Jam event, fans will witness at least one round of racing as trucks compete for the points that can take them to the World Finals.

In head-to-head racing, two trucks face off around the track in each of several rounds of a tournament. When the dust settles, the winner will claim the most points.

Some events feature a "Chicago-style" race where two trucks start out on opposite sides of the track and chase each other around for one lightning lap. These ultrafast showdowns stack up from qualifying runs through semifinals and into a winner-takes-all championship.

Monster Jam events also frequently feature timed obstacle-course runs where only the fastest competitors can claim the vital points. Look out too for the Monster Jam Triple Threat Series which features side-by-side races by Monster Jam's signature Speedsters and ATVs working to achieve speed supremacy.

# Fearsome FREESTYLE

**F**or some of the wildest action and biggest tricks in the world of Monster Jam, the name of the game is freestyle.

In these trick-heavy competitions, Monster Jam trucks take to the course for 120 seconds of pure fury. Making jumps, crushing cars, doing donuts, popping wheelies, and achieving backflips are only part of the madness.

When a Monster Jam truck finishes its freestyle run, every fan in the stadium/arena can go online, input their scores between 1-10 and the competitor receives the average score. Some trucks even earn a perfect score of ten!

But that's not all! Many Monster Jam events include individually scored donut and wheelie competitions, so make sure you don't leave until the very end!

# ATHLETES
## at the Wheel

Meet some of the greatest athletes in Monster Jam history!

### Tom Meents

The only eleven-time World Champion in the sport has more than earned his daredevil reputation in Monster Jam history. Tom Meents is known across the globe for his cutting-edge style and his need to get major air. He's also broken more ground on long-range jumps and Monster Jam truck flips than any other athlete. In his truck Max-D, it's only a matter of time until Meents adds to his winning streak.

### Colton & Jared Eichelberger

While Tom Meents has trained plenty of athletes at Monster Jam University, he's most proud of his own sons: athletes Colton and Jared Eichelberger. Since joining Monster Jam in 2014 Colton has risen to the occasion, even besting his dad in competition! Meanwhile, Jared has been training to match the family's daredevil style with a few signature tricks of his own.

## Dennis Anderson

Describing his style as "rough and reckless with a lot of carnage," athlete Dennis Anderson is a Monster Jam driving legend. Competing for thirty-five years with his fan favorite creation Grave Digger, Anderson is known for his nonstop style and multiple championships. Once he gets going on the track, Dennis won't stop until the fans are on their feet or until Grave Digger gives out on him—whichever comes first.

## Adam, Ryan, & Krysten Anderson

An Anderson has dominated Monster Jam for decades, and that won't be changing anytime soon. That's because Dennis's three grown children all compete on the Monster Jam tour! Adam has won multiple racing and freestyle championships, including back-to-back racing honors in 2013 and 2014. Ryan takes the legacy of Grave Digger forward with his extremely popular Son-Uva Digger truck, which won the 2017 Monster Jam World Finals Racing Championship. Krysten Anderson was originally interested in designing truck bodies for Monster Jam, but when she was invited to become an athlete in 2017, she jumped at the chance to live up to the family name.

# Are You Ready to ROLL?

If you're strapped into the seat of a Monster Jam truck, you better hope that you learned everything Monster Jam University had to teach you. To make sure you can take it to the next level, here's an epic final exam.

**1** How much dirt does it take to create the field of play at a Monster Jam event? _____

**2** How long is a standard Monster Jam freestyle round? _____

**3** Who's known as the "Professor" of Monster Jam University?

_____

**4** What holds the athlete steady in the seat of their Monster Jam truck?

_____

**5** What great American city gives its name to Monster Jam's style of chaselike racing event?

______________________

**6** What is the highest possible score a Monster Jam truck can earn in a freestyle competition?

______________________

**7** How much do average Monster Jam truck tires weigh? ______________________

**8** Complete this essential Monster Jam truck driving rule: "When in doubt,

______________________."

**9** The ultra-detailed features on a Monster Jam truck body are also called what?

______________________

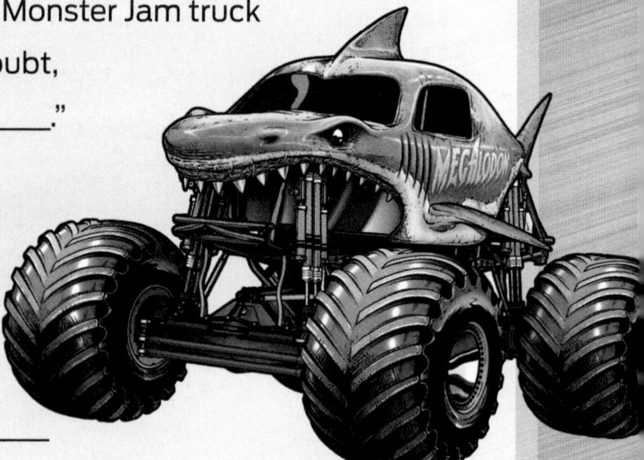

**10** How many horsepower does the average Monster Jam engine produce? ______________________

Answers: 1: 7,500 tons; 2: 120 seconds; 3: Tom Meents; 4: five-point harness; 5: Chicago; 6: forty points; 7: 800–900 pounds; 8: throttle out; 9: bolt-ons; 10: 1,500

# Meet The

# MONSTER JAM

# SUPERSTARS

**M**ore than mere automotive equipment, the Monster Jam trucks are like living, breathing beasts—all with their eyes on the prize. From their custom 3D fiberglass bodies to their epic histories, each Monster Jam truck has a personality and power all its own. Read on to find your favorite!

# GRAVE DIGGER

## THE GRAVEYARD GOODS

* There are a total of nine Grave Diggers on tour and each one of them is hand-painted. It takes 60 hours to paint each one.

* Thanks to their high-speed style, Team Digger has won a record seven Racing championships at the Monster Jam World Finals.

* Grave Digger accomplished the impossible at the Monster Jam World Finals XVII by winning a true "Double Down" with victories in both the 2016 World Racing championship *and* the 2016 World Freestyle championship!

The biggest star in Monster Jam history buries the competition. Thundering out of its home base in Kill Devil Hills, North Carolina, Grave Digger takes no prisoners. A fan-favorite Monster Jam truck champion for thirty-five years, the Digger is known for its unique design. This legend is built on a gruesome green chassis with headlights that beam out like blood-red eyes. Its ghostly graveyard paint job includes the tombstones of the many trucks it's defeated over the years.

## SCIENCE JAM

To achieve the proper launch velocity for a jump, a 12,000-pound truck like Grave Digger needs to go from zero to thirty miles per hour in only 1.52 seconds!

But it's not just style that makes this Monster Jam truck so popular. Grave Digger is a true speed demon. Creator Dennis Anderson pioneered the full-throttle method of Monster Jam racing, hitting every jump and trick with his pedal to the metal. Today, every athlete on Team Digger knows that burying your competitor begins with burying the needle of your speedometer.

# The Legend of Grave Digger

The legend of Grave Digger began in 1982. Other racers made fun of athlete Dennis Anderson for tinkering with a rundown 1951 Ford panel truck. But he boldly joked to his critics, "I'll take this old junk and dig you a grave with it!"

The finished vehicle rode high with a menacing red body, but Grave Digger advanced quickly. Within two years, a blue-and-silver behemoth spread the Digger name across the country. In 1985, the truck was updated once more with its best-known ghostly design, as Anderson's no-holds-barred driving style toppled all the other trucks in its league.

Today, the entire Anderson clan keeps a fleet of Grave Diggers and develops new Monster Jam truck technology in their home, the aptly named Digger's Dungeon. In addition to Dennis, Team Digger athletes include his children, Ryan, Adam, and Krysten, who made her Monster Jam debut in 2017. From start to finish, taking the wheel of Grave Digger is truly a family affair.

**G**rinding up the Monster Jam track and pushing the Grave Digger dynasty forward is the roaring Son-uva Digger. Its highly detailed graveyard paint job delivers a dark, dangerous take on Dad's original look.

No bones about it, this is one intimidating opponent. Since Ryan Anderson debuted Son-uva Digger in 2011, the Monster Jam truck has been on a hot streak, appearing in five straight World Finals. And in 2017, Son-uva Digger proved that the apple doesn't fall far from the tree, scooping up the Monster Jam World Finals Racing Championship.

The competitor at the very height of Monster Jam's international battles takes everything to the max! The futuristic SUV best known as Max-D is a fiery steel behemoth ready to tear apart anything that gets in its way. But its spiky design isn't just for raw crushing power and major intimidation. Max-D is actually one of the most aerodynamic and fastest Monster Jam trucks, winning six Racing and five Freestyle Championships.

Tearing apart expectations, Max-D also holds the honor of being the most innovative vehicle out there. Each year, this creator of chaos invents higher and longer jumps and pushes the art of the truck flip to the extreme. With its full-throttle style, Max-D will go down in history as the truck that changed Monster Jam driving forever.

## MAXIMUM DOMINATION

* Under athlete Tom Meents, Max-D and its forebears have won more World Finals championships than any other truck or athlete.

* Meents isn't content to rest on Max-D's past accomplishments: The athlete and his truck are constantly innovating new kinds of tricks, like the amazing front flip.

* In 2015, Tom became the first to ever successfully land the Double Backflip.

* Records were meant to be broken, like in 2016 when Max-D jumped over six other Monster Jam trucks!

# The Evolution of Max-D

**J**ust like its ever-expanding repertoire of awe-inspiring tricks, Max-D's look has evolved over the decades.

When World Champion athlete Tom Meents debuted the Monster Jam truck originally known as Maximum Destruction, its flaming-hot art style made the truck body look like a piece of molten steel straight from the forge.

However, that wasn't wild enough. The main Max-D body soon grew into a major metal monster. With its signature spikes and the Max-D creature character ready to rip out of its body, the classic look of the Monster Jam champ was firmly established.

And as the Max-D team has expanded to include the likes of athletes Neil Elliott and Tom Meents' sons, Colton and Jared Eichelberger, the look evolved. Fans have been wowed by limited-run special versions of the truck like the Max-D Gold Edition.

# The Rivalry  VS.

Like the titans of any great sport, Grave Digger and Max-D have developed an intense rivalry over their years in Monster Jam. The roots of these on-the-track grudge matches stretch back to the very first Monster Jam World Finals where athletes Tom Meents and Dennis Anderson split honors in racing and freestyle. The athletes remain friends off the field, but on the track they're archrivals.

And no place is that rivalry felt more strongly than at the Monster Jam World Finals. Aside from being the two most decorated vehicles in the history of the championship, Max-D and Grave Digger have often gone turn for turn. In World Finals VII, Anderson and Meents kicked off the Racing competition with Grave Digger pulling out a photo-finish victory on its way to the top prize. But Max-D roared back in the freestyle competition, beating its rival for the championship by just four points. The athletes went head-to-head in the World Finals XI Racing Championship with Grave Digger narrowly winning out.

In recent years, Grave Digger has been at an all-time peak level of performance, but Max-D is never far behind on the track, and Meents remains the sport's most decorated athlete. So it's anybody's guess who will launch to victory the next time these Monster Jam titans square off.

The top two Monster Jam trucks on the planet are only the tip of the iceberg. Some of the biggest names in the sport are vehicles whose looks and driving styles range from massively mythological to downright dangerous. From their horns and scales to their hooks and claws, these Monster Jam all-stars make racers sleep with one eye open.

# El Toro Loco

**C**harging into Monster Jam in 2001, the smoke-spitting El Toro Loco made its name on the track with the rage of a stampeding bull.

One of the very first Monster Jam trucks with a custom-designed 3D body shell, the signature horns of this snorting monster drive through obstacles like a wild bulldozer. And the athletes behind the horns know that El Toro Loco has a crazy reputation to live up to. Whether they're popping massive wheelies like the rearing runs of the truck's namesake or trampling over scores of crushed cars, the many Toros in Monster Jam are always a sight to behold.

So just how *loco* is El Toro Loco? Let's find out.

## SCIENCE JAM

People who are as angry as El Toro Loco are said to be "seeing red" because bullfighting bulls were traditionally taunted with red capes. But in truth, bulls can't even see red or almost any color at all! Like most mammals, they're largely color-blind.

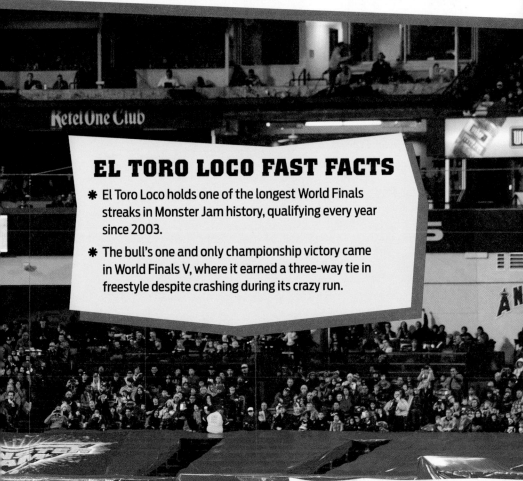

## EL TORO LOCO FAST FACTS

* El Toro Loco holds one of the longest World Finals streaks in Monster Jam history, qualifying every year since 2003.

* The bull's one and only championship victory came in World Finals V, where it earned a three-way tie in freestyle despite crashing during its crazy run.

# ZOMBIE<sup>SM</sup>

**T**his crowd-pleasing Monster Jam truck is anything but undead. In fact, Zombie shambles, scrambles, and shreds its way through the field with its signature rotting limbs clawing all the way. This Monster Jam truck's signature look combines the sagging skin of a graveyard ghoul with bright-pink BRAAAAAAINS and realistic features like teeth, arms, and even hair thrown in.

Introduced as part of a contest that invited fans to name the next Monster Jam superstar, this bug-eyed brain eater won the vote by a mile. And since it hit the track in 2013, crowds have cheered for the competitor that "came back from the dead" like no other.

But Zombie isn't satisfied with being just for show. Since its debut, the infection has spread, with multiple Zombie trucks competing nationally and working together in the World Finals XVI Freestyle encore to wow the crowd. Could this be the start of a full-on Zombie apocalypse? We can only hope so.

# BLUE THUNDER ®

**W**hen this supercharged Monster Jam truck takes to the track, get ready to watch sparks fly!

One of the longest-running competitors in the world of Monster Jam, Blue Thunder cuts an unmistakable figure with its shockingly slick paint job. This electrified warrior is driven to win through a mixture of pure energy and powerful fury.

Aside from striking a white-hot presence on the track, Blue Thunder cracked through the crowded, cloudy field of play to win victories at home and abroad. It drove for glory in the World Finals Racing championship in 2001 and again in the Double Down Showdown Racing Final in 2013, proving that lightning does in fact strike twice.

And who knows when it'll strike next? Predicting Blue Thunder's next move is like catching lighting in a bottle. Whatever happens, we're sure its engine's thunderous roar will make your hair stand on end.

## SCIENCE JAM

Thunder can be heard when superhot lightning bolts strike the sky. The lightning causes a quick change in air temperature and pressure, making the clouds crackle like a small sonic boom.

**Pirate's Curse**™

**A**vast, me hearties! Make way for the roughest, toughest cutthroat on the Monster Jam circuit.

Bobbing up and down on the obstacle course like a dreaded pirate ship of old, Pirate's Curse cuts as scary a figure as any boat that ever flew the Jolly Roger flag. With its trusty cutlass in one hand and a razor-sharp hook replacing the other, this Monster Jam truck is ready to cut the competition down to size.

A recent addition to the world of Monster Jam, this renegade quickly won its very first race after sailing in from "The Dark Sea." Since then, Pirate's Curse has racked up multiple wins including an international championship run in Australia. Keep yer trophies close, Monster Jam trucks, lest this pirate make scallywags of any and all that dare cross its path!

DRAGON ℠

Like the fire-breathing beast of fantasy, this epic creature screeches across Monster Jam competitions, striking fear into the heart of anyone who dares to oppose it.

The scaly body of Dragon represents a tough hide and an even tougher competitor. With bolted-on horns and wings, it's no surprise that the flame-wielding monster has burned its brand into the minds and hearts of fans. This Monster Jam truck of mythic size can shoot fire from its nose when called upon in exhibitions.

And just like its namesake, Dragon has soared to untold heights since debuting in Monster Jam. Best known as the undisputed Double Down Showdown champion in World Finals XVII, the great green goliath is still spreading its wings. When this Dragon reaches its full potential, it will scorch its name across the Monster Jam history books.

# Formidable FEATURES

From beastly bolt-ons to interactive extensions, these are the coolest Monster Jam body features ever to shake up the sport.

You might think the iconic horns of El Toro Loco are its greatest feature, and you might be right. But also in the running are this Monster Jam star's steaming "nostrils" that heat up the air like the maddest bull to ever charge the ring.

The Monster Jam truck known as Monster Mutt shares more than an animal instinct with its canine brethren. From nose to tail, the bolt-ons for every model of Mutt show off its teeth-gritting, tail-wagging, ear-twitching displays of dominance. Beware! This dog does bite!

Whipping and gripping their way through the air alongside Zombie are a pair of arms that are bloody, blistered, and breathtaking to behold. The undead from your favorite scary movie may lurch to life, but when these arms come for the competition, they won't be moving so slowly!

The Monster Jam standout Scooby-Doo! may take its name from the famed canine, but this cartoon collar is a work of art all its own. The truck's dog tag clangs around with every jump and jostle.

The massive Mohawk atop Mohawk Warrior is more than just a signature hairstyle. In truth, this hair is aerodynamics in action—cutting down the wind resistance so Mohawk Warrior can speed its way to an epic victory.

Aside from its scaly exterior, Dragon can breathe fire in massive bursts that singe the air all around the arena and send even the bravest competitors running for the hills.

# MEGALODON

B a dum. Ba da dum. Ba dum. Ba dum. Ba dum.

Competitors had better watch the waters! The mighty Megalodon was named for the ancient and terrifying creature of the deep, and once it hits the track, this four-wheeled shark won't stop biting its way through the dirt and dust until it tastes victory.

From its sinister fins to its beady black eyes, Megalodon's fiberglass shell stands out as one of the most detailed in Monster Jam history. And as the cool blue body of the great fish cuts its way across the track like a predator in search of its next meal, you better believe that its wide open mouth will find prey very soon.

47

# EarthShaker

When Monster Jam's team of track designers want to build up the biggest, baddest obstacles imaginable, they call on the likes of EarthShaker.

Modeled after the heavy-duty construction vehicles that help build the Monster Jam track, this bruiser gets the job done. And EarthShaker is already rattling the foundation of the sport in honor of the dump trucks that came before it—having hauled home the top prize at the 2017 Double Down Showdown.

Whether it's building up a victory in a high-flying freestyle competition or tearing down a row of car obstacles, EarthShaker understands that the job of winning a championship is like any other job. It can only be done with good old-fashioned hard work.

MOHAWK WARRIOR

A shock of spiky black hair would stand out anywhere, but on the tracks of Monster Jam, the towering tuft of Mohawk Warrior astonishes fans.

Behind a pair of opaque shades, the high-style warrior riding the side of this Monster Jam truck raises one eyebrow as if to say, "Try me." And luckily, this sleek vehicle has the speed and savagery to back up its look.

When this one-of-a-kind competitor debuted with a splash at World Finals XI, Mohawk Warrior immediately earned legions of fans willing to slick up their hair thanks to an "anything goes" style of driving. Perhaps nothing shows off this attitude better than the truck's freestyle run at World Finals XIII, where the Warrior became the first ever to complete two consecutive backflips. And the best part of all? When the flips were done and the dust had settled, its hair was still perfectly intact.

# TEAM HOT WHEELS FIRESTORM

For nearly fifty years, Mattel's Hot Wheels has been leading the way in the world of collectible cars and trucks. But with the real-life Team Hot Wheels Firestorm Monster Jam truck, the company also broke new ground in real automotive science.

During competition, Team Hot Wheels Firestorm delivers on its forward-thinking design with no-nonsense driving. This style has taken it to five straight World Finals—including World Finals XVIII, where it became the first Monster Jam truck to nail four backflips in one freestyle run.

# THE AMAZING AMAZON

* WONDER WOMAN™ first appeared in *All Star Comics* #8 before starring in *Sensation Comics*.
* WONDER WOMAN's classic Super-Villains include CHEETAH, SILVER SWAN, ARES, and CIRCE.

For over seventy-five years, evil forces everywhere have quaked at the name of one astounding Super Hero: WONDER WOMAN! Now the powerful Amazon Warrior has inspired her own Monster Jam truck to carry her mission forward.

WONDER WOMAN has served as an inspiration to fans worldwide through comic books, TV shows, and movies, and her Monster Jam truck represents her greatest qualities. The red stands for her boundless courage. The yellow recalls her Golden LASSO OF TRUTH. And the silver shines like her bullet-deflecting bracelets.

When the WONDER WOMAN Monster Jam truck takes to the track, it will fly high above its competitors . . . without the help of her INVISIBLE JET.

# GIRL Power

The women of Monster Jam bring power and precision to the track!

## Becky McDonough

Starting out as a technician, Becky McDonough eventually rose to become Crew Chief before getting behind the wheel. Her road to the seat of a Monster Jam truck may have had a few twists, but her drive toward victory is unmistakable.

## Ami Houde

Driving behind the wheel of Zombie may give you an undead appearance on the track, but Ami Houde is all energy. This athlete came to Monster Jam already a motor sport dynamo as a twenty-five-year motocross veteran from a family of champion bike racers. And since strapping into the big chair of Monster Jam, she's brought adrenaline-fueled skills to the sport alongside her dedicated practice regimen, making her a force that won't quit.

## Brianna Mahon

An athlete with equal parts grit and grace, Brianna Mahon brings a phenomenal skill set to Team SCOOBY-DOO! A former dancer and dirt-track-racing enthusiast, Mahon made a splash at her first World Finals in 2016 by wowing the crowd with a flawless backflip, and she hasn't looked back since.

## Bailey Shea

A speed demon at heart, SCOOBY-DOO! athlete Bailey Shea zoomed her way into Monster Jam after ten years as a professional ATV racer. That experience makes her the perfect competitor for the lightning-fast races of Monster Jam's Triple Threat series.

# GIRL Power

This Monster Mutt Dalmatian athlete is a fan favorite across the globe. That's not just because Candice Jolly loves to travel, but because she has a competitive streak that runs beyond Monster Jam to hobbies like sport fishing and horseback riding. And at each competition, Candice leaves her mark on the track, starting with the ritual of wearing crazy colorful socks for good luck. We don't think she'll need it!

## Cynthia Gauthier

A former Monster Jam crew member who rose to the role of athlete, Cynthia Gauthier knows her Monster Mutt Dalmatian truck inside and out. And on the track, this French-Canadian maverick gives it her all and leaves everything on the field.

## Myranda Cozad

This member of Team SCOOBY-DOO! brings a little bit of racing fury to the big show in every competition. Myranda Cozad is an ATV diehard when she's off duty, but behind the wheel at Monster Jam, she loves to size up her showmanship by grabbing big air. A onetime fan who rose to the pro level, Cozad is always ready to spread the Monster Jam love wherever she goes.

## Krysten Anderson

Don't sleep on this revved-up newcomer just because her father and brothers have torn up the Monster Jam circuit before her. Krysten Anderson is her own breed of competitor in the seat of Grave Digger, where her creative style delivers a showy, memorable bag of tricks on the track. Once you've seen this Anderson drive, you won't soon forget her.

# THE MYSTERY MACHINE

* Step aside, Fred and Shaggy! In the world of Monster Jam, SCOOBY-DOO! is ruled by an all-star, all-women driving team.

* The character of SCOOBY-DOO! is a Great Dane, a breed of dog so large it has been known to tower over some people . . . just like his Monster Jam truck counterpart!

* In his animated adventures, SCOOBY-DOO! has teamed up with countless entertainment icons!

# SCOOBY-DOO!

Tumbling out of spooky, ghost-ridden hills full of creaky haunted mansions comes the greatest mystery-solver of all time: SCOOBY-DOO! For years, this colorful Monster Jam truck has embodied the cartoon canine on the track from nose to tail. Add on Scooby-Doo's signature SD tag and wide grin, and it's easy to see why fans everywhere are eating up this custom-built mutt like a box of SCOOBY SNACKS.

This Monster Jam truck has landed at World Finals repeatedly in recent years including a wow-worthy performance of a flawless backflip in 2016 that leaves no mystery to the truck's competitive nature.

# MONSTER MUTT®

**F**or many Monster Jam fans, the original dog is still the top dog. Barking its way through the arena for over a decade, Monster Mutt is beloved for its unleashed style of competing. With its signature snout, sharp teeth, ears, and tail, it runs wild in freestyle and snaps through races faster than a greyhound. That gnarly feel inspires fans everywhere to throw on a Monster Mutt cap and howl in triumph.

And triumph has come for the original Monster Mutt. The master mongrel took a runaway victory in the freestyle championship at World Finals XI in 2010, leaving many other competitors in the doghouse with the highest score possible.

# Mutt-Tastic

**I**f you thought one Monster Mutt was awesome enough, then prepare yourself for a Monster Jam dog pile!

In addition to the original four-legged howler, Monster Mutt Dalmatian and Monster Mutt Rottweiler bring their savage style to competitions to make for a true pack of wild things. Here's how these Monster Mutts back up their bark.

With a fierce team of female athletes and a spotted look that's

unmistakable, Monster Mutt Dalmatian is digging its way through the hottest Monster Jam competitions. And with its signature coat wowing fans everywhere, the truck has inspired the beloved Dalmatian Nation Fashion Show at Pit Parties worldwide.

Joining the famed Dog Pound Team after a massive fan vote, Monster Mutt Rottweiler delivers on the fierce reputation of its namesake. Revving up its engine like a dog unchained, Rottweiler gnawed into its first World Finals in 2014.

With pinpoint steering powered by its namesake, the Lucas Oil Crusader is a Monster Jam truck ready to get straight-up medieval. With the slashing, crashing driving style of a knight jousting toward victory, this competitor claims one of the sturdiest bodies in the sport. And that armored-up appearance helps the Lucas Oil Crusader remain a valiant veteran of many battles.

Constantly hitting World Finals since its debut in 2011, the Monster Jam truck has made it all the way to the semifinals in competition, proving that someday its steel sword will feel the heat of a championship.

## SCIENCE JAM

The most important quality of motor oil is its viscosity, or thickness. Oil in a Monster Jam truck engine gets thicker when it gets cold and thinner when hot, but its unique viscosity allows it to protect engine parts even when the competition gets superheated!

# SOLDIER FORTUNE

**W**hen this tanklike competitor joined the Monster Jam fight in 2015, fans everywhere stood up to salute.

Soldier Fortune isn't just a rugged military Monster Jam truck, it's also a living tribute to the men and women who serve the United States at home and abroad. And to date, this vehicle has served with crowd-pleasing distinction.

# SOLDIER FORTUNE

## BLACK OPS

**A**rriving under cover of night, the competition won't even see this stealthy vehicle coming. A covert competitor running alongside its sister soldier, the Monster Jam truck known as Soldier Fortune Black Ops can strike anyplace, anytime.

# N.E.A.
## NEW EARTH AUTHORITY
# POLICE

After fighting crime in the future, this chrome-finished Monster Jam truck arrived in our world to promote peace through policing.

But the New Earth Authority (also known as the N.E.A. Police) is more than a futuristic slice of utopian engineering. Its domelike structure gives it additional speed on the track as well as the ability to roll back from any spinout like an unstoppable high-tech squad car.

And as long as N.E.A. Police continues to shine its bright blue chassis in the name of truth and justice, the competition will have nowhere to hide.

ALIEN

# INVASION™

ook to the night skies, and you might just catch a glimpse of the official UFO of Monster Jam.

Alien Invasion glows with the eerie green power of fifty feet of LED lighting built right into its otherworldly body, and that's just the beginning. By the time this spaceship-like Monster Jam truck lands, you'll be staring into the ominous black windshield, wondering exactly what's on the other side.

With a rocket-powered readiness, Alien Invasion flew straight into World Finals XVII before capturing its first racing title across the globe in Manila, Philippines, later that year. Looks like Alien Invasion is poised for a world takeover of Monster Jam.

The major Monster Jam trucks may be the stars of the show, but they're hardly the only excitement fans can find in the arena. That's where the quick, compact vehicles of the Triple Threat Series come in.

As part of this popular Monster Jam tour, athletes kick things off by racing separate events on superfast Speedsters and souped-up ATVs modeled after their main Monster Jam trucks.

Speedsters are specially modified utility task vehicles. These compact off-road zoom buggies get their kicks thanks to 110-horsepower engines that allow competitors to achieve top speeds on obstacle-filled tracks. Athletes guide their Speedsters in both racing

# Speedsters and ATVs

and obstacle-based competitions, navigating hairpin turns that even big trucks like Grave Digger and El Toro Loco can't match.

The Triple Threat Series continues with an all-out showdown on ATVs. But these Monster Jam all-terrain vehicles are unlike any four-wheelers you've ever seen. Decked out with aerodynamic panels in the style of Monster Jam trucks like Max-D and N.E.A. Police, these ATVs force racers to elbow one another out of the way on a path where only one of eight competitors can claim victory.

With these down and dirty models speeding past at a head-spinning pace, Speedsters and ATVs alike have earned their place in Monster Jam.

# NORTHERN Nightmare

triking out of the Great White North, this Canadian crusher has given the maple leaf a menacing reputation in Monster Jam. Northern Nightmare rolled into the sport hard in 2011 like an icy wind, and it soon established Canada's claim to fame with Monster Jam World Freestyle championship in 2012. Now the competition bows down to this native hero.

# FS1

L ining up like the gridiron greats that inspired it, FS1 Cleatus is the ultimate down and dirty competitor. Emblazoned with the robotic mascot of Fox Sports, this tough-as-nails truck is always ready when it's crunch time. FS1 Cleatus is proving you don't need armor-plated shoulder pads to drive other Monster Jam trucks back on their heels. The truck made it to World Finals during its very first year on the circuit— an incredible feat for a new team.

# THE VP Racing FUELS MAD SCIENTIST

It's alive! Running onto the track with wild eyes and even wilder technology, the VP Racing Fuels Mad Scientist is the ultimate creation from a cutting-edge company. VP Racing Fuels is known for fuels and additives that make engines run faster, stronger, and smoother. And this Monster Jam ruck is living up to that reputation, having won 2017 Monster Jam World Finals Freestyle competition with the first ever completed front flip!

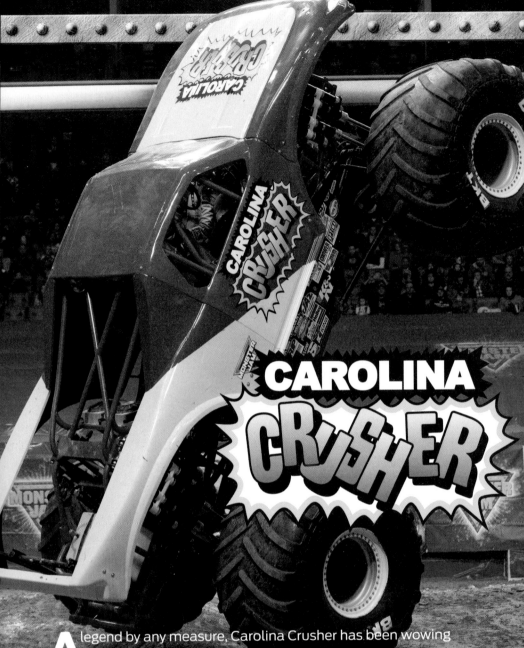

# CAROLINA CRUSHER

**A** legend by any measure, Carolina Crusher has been wowing Monster Jam fans for over thirty years. From its earliest days on the circuit, this red-and-yellow Chevy has showed that it has what it takes to compete against any truck the world over. And though it's been years since the Crusher's rivalry with Grave Digger has calmed down, this truck's resurgence in modern Monster Jam means that absolutely anything can happen in the years ahead.

# Monster Jam Advancements

**O**nce upon a time, Monster Jam took the idea of a car-crushing truck and evolved it into a world-class, gravity-defying sport. Today, it's still at work evolving its vehicles beyond the future of automotive technology.

Normal cars and trucks still clunk along on leaf springs—a suspension system that can crumble if you hit the curb too hard. Monster Jam trucks pioneered the use of coilover shocks—super-tough, thick springs infused with nitrogen gas to provide up to thirty inches of travel. These protect Monster Jam trucks from breaking after big-air jumps.

Even the strongest competitor can be whipped pretty hard by a Monster Jam truck flip, but thanks in part to the next generation of the Neck and Head Restraint, their safety is always assured. HANS stands for Head And Neck Support, and this lifesaver is like a super-hard neck pillow made of carbon fibers that locks an athlete's helmet in place for even the roughest Monster Jam tricks.

81

# Monster Jam's Next Generation

**M**ore than anything, Monster Jam is always on the hunt for its next great athlete, and each year all-new young competitors get behind the wheel for a chance at glory.

The 2017 class from Monster Jam University is one of the hottest to ever hit the road on the Monster Jam tour. Fans everywhere have thrilled at the energy these rookies are bringing to the sport and to some of the most legendary Monster Jam trucks.

Included in this next generation are athletes like Krysten Anderson who broke ground as the first female athlete to drive Grave Digger. J. R.

Seasock, son of acclaimed athlete John Seasock, also continued the family legacy as he took on the task of piloting Monster Mutt Rottweiler. Meanwhile, longtime fan and former EMT Armando Castro trained day and night to harness the fiery fury of El Toro Loco. A skilled athlete and performer who has traveled the globe, Bernard Lyght took his driving to another world behind the wheel of Alien Invasion. Ami Houde became the latest Canadian sensation to rock the sport from the athlete's seat of Zombie. And Camden Murphy of NASCAR fame sits behind the wheel of Pirate's Curse on the Monster Jam Triple Threat Tour.

But the road to triumph has one important pit stop for these new talents: the Double Down Showdown. Held every year as the kick-start competition of Monster Jam World Finals, the Showdown pits the newest athletes against one another for a chance to compete in the World Racing and Freestyle championships. Which of these next-generation athletes will rise to the occasion? Keep an eye on the Double Down Showdown to watch the action happen!

# Design Your Own
# Monster Jam Truck

**W**ith their radical, unforgettable designs, Monster Jam trucks represent the spirit of their athletes and the passion of their fans. So what better way to celebrate the ingenuity of the Monster Jam world than by designing a truck all your own?

Start by choosing a name that describes you. Are you a no-nonsense bruiser? A do-gooding gladiator? Something in between? Build your new truck by adding words from our inspiration bank below, or cook up a totally new name by yourself!

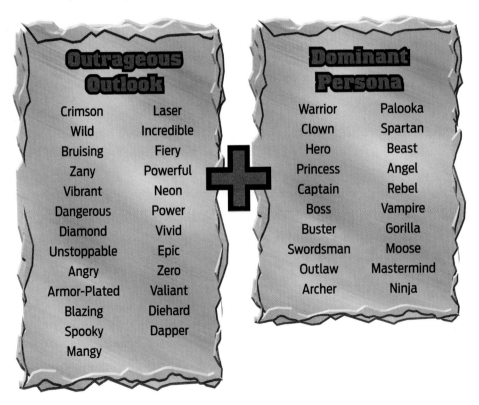

## Outrageous Outlook

| | |
|---|---|
| Crimson | Laser |
| Wild | Incredible |
| Bruising | Fiery |
| Zany | Powerful |
| Vibrant | Neon |
| Dangerous | Power |
| Diamond | Vivid |
| Unstoppable | Epic |
| Angry | Zero |
| Armor-Plated | Valiant |
| Blazing | Diehard |
| Spooky | Dapper |
| Mangy | |

## Dominant Persona

| | |
|---|---|
| Warrior | Palooka |
| Clown | Spartan |
| Hero | Beast |
| Princess | Angel |
| Captain | Rebel |
| Boss | Vampire |
| Buster | Gorilla |
| Swordsman | Moose |
| Outlaw | Mastermind |
| Archer | Ninja |

## My Monster Jam Name Is:

Once you know your name, start building up the bolt-ons that will make your truck's style come alive. Copy parts from the bank below or design your amazing additions in a sketchbook. The sky's the limit!

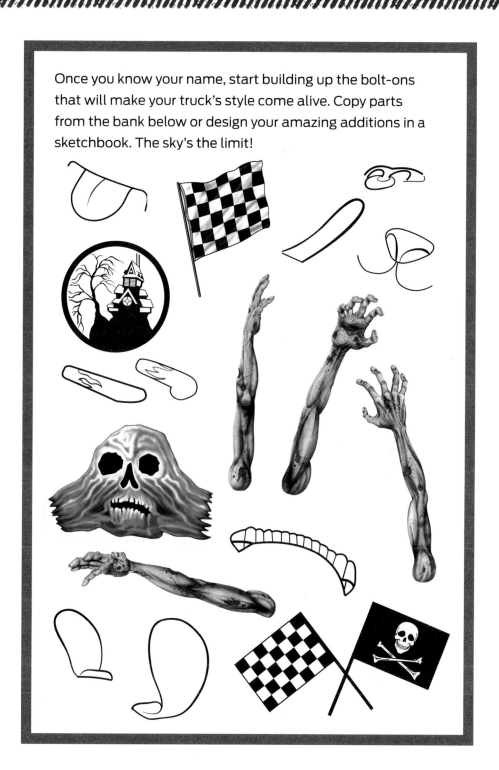

# Design Your Own Monster Jam Truck

Once you know your truck's name and what you stand for, design the body of your Monster Jam truck on the pages below or photocopy these to make an entire army of trucks!

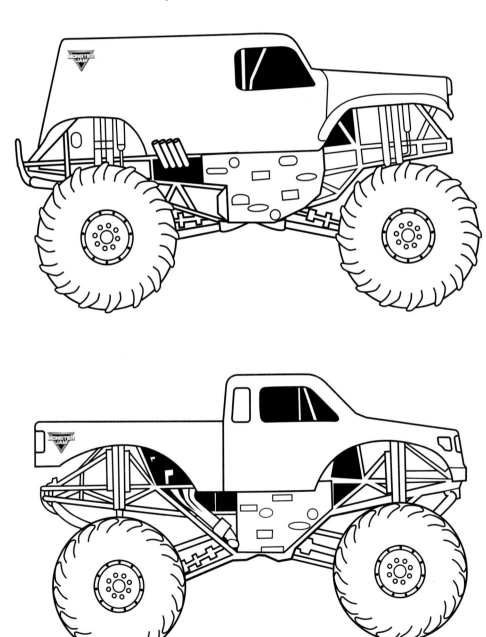

86

# Design Your Own Monster Jam Truck

Your Monster Jam truck is going to be seeing a lot of action, so get used to drawing and coloring it from every angle as it races to the World Finals!

88

Once you have a Monster Jam truck ready to unleash on the world, you'll have to build it a daring, difficult track for both racing and freestyle. Check out these automotive obstacles that you can draw into your own track design along with ramps, competitors, and, of course, a massive audience!

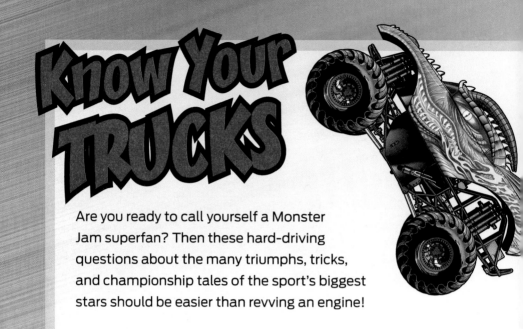

# Know Your TRUCKS

Are you ready to call yourself a Monster Jam superfan? Then these hard-driving questions about the many triumphs, tricks, and championship tales of the sport's biggest stars should be easier than revving an engine!

**1** How many Monster Jam trucks did Max-D jump over in 2016? _____

**2** Which Monster Jam truck is named for an ancient undersea creature? _____

**3** Which Monster Jam truck won both the 2016 World Racing championship and the World Freestyle championship?

_____

**4** What year did Grave Digger debut?

_____

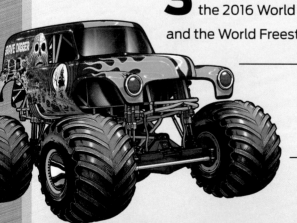

**5** Which fan-favorite Monster Jam athlete spent ten years as a pro ATV racer? _____

**6** Who won the Double Down Showdown at Monster Jam World Finals XVII? _____

**7** Monster Jam Speedsters are what kind of vehicle? _____

**8** Monster Mutt won which Monster Jam World Final championship and when? _____

**9** Where do new athletes to the Monster Jam world compete to make it into the World Finals? _____

**10** What Monster Jam truck made its world debut at the World Finals XI? _____ _____

Answers: 1: six trucks; 2: Megalodon; 3: Grave Digger; 4: 1982; 5: Bailey Shea; 6: Dragon; 7: utility task vehicle; 8: Freestyle championship in 2010; 9: the Double Down Showdown; 10: Mohawk Warrior

# MONSTER JAM
# THE BIG SHOW

**T**he world of Monster Jam is about more than getting big air and making big noise.

With each new competition in every season, Monster Jam trucks compete for points in racing, freestyle, and other feats of skill. But only one competitor in each show will drive off with a mighty Monster Jam trophy. These steel works of art are offering not only bragging rights but also a chance for their winners to make it to the big one: World Finals in Las Vegas, Nevada.

An old Monster Jam saying declares of these titans, "To thy legion cry, thou shall arise of flames and thunder to claim thy prize." Read on to see the path Monster Jam trucks take to the biggest stage of the year and beyond.

# Monster Jam
# TOURS

## Monster Jam Triple Threat Series

In the marathon of the Monster Jam Triple Threat Series, eight Triple Threat athletes start out with lightning fast "Chicago Style" racing followed by sky-scraping wheelies! Next comes action-packed ATV racing followed by the head-spinning Monster Jam donut contest, Speedster obstacle course, and, last but not least, Monster Jam Freestyle! When the dust settles, only one ultimate champion can claim the trophy and the high-point total on the line.

## FS1 Championship & Stadium Series

Perhaps the most competitive series of the year, the two tours of the FS1 Championship and Stadium Series each feature fourteen top Monster Jam trucks. Traditional freestyle and racing events are key, though athletes must hit qualifying times to race in each new town, with winners in each contest earning fourteen points. At tours' end, only the top point-earner locks in a World Finals bid.

## Arena Events

Going far beyond your usual exhibition event, Monster Jam arena tours bring the wildest action seen all year long. Teams of athletes dedicated to each of eight epic Monster Jam trucks throw down in quick challenges of skill. There are traditional racing and freestyle events with bursts of ATV racing thrown in. Best of all, arena shows feature unique trick competitions focused only on donuts and wheelies.

## Double Down Showdown

When the season wraps, next generation Monster Jam trucks and up-and-coming athletes alike get their chance for glory. The Double Down Showdown kicks off the World Finals weekend with sixteen racers new to the championship competing for the last spot in the finals. This cutthroat competition with the newest stars of the sport is always one of the most exciting stops all year long.

# CLASSIC MATCHUPS

**E**ach year as competitions heat up across Monster Jam tours, new rivalries explode when icons and upstarts collide on the track. Here are four modern Monster Jam showdowns to watch.

## Son-Uva Digger vs. Team Hot Wheels Firestorm

Over the past several years, Son-Uva Digger athlete and Monster Jam legacy Ryan Anderson has been on an unstoppable hot streak capped off by two runner-up performances in the World Finals. But quick on Son-Uva's heels has been Team Hot Wheels Firestorm, driven primarily by the ever-impressive wow-factor moments of Scott Buetow. It's a close race to see who can claim a title first.

## Max-D vs. El Toro Loco

For years, Monster Jam fans have been faced with one tough question: spikes or horns? That's because Max-D and El Toro Loco each draw massive amounts of onlookers to their cause every time they square off. From Detroit to Las Vegas and back again, this pair of legends has gone neck and neck on the Monster Jam tour, ever beating back the other in the season point totals. No matter who wins in the long run, both competitors are pushing each other to new heights.

## Monster Mutt Dalmatian vs. SCOOBY-DOO!

It's a dog-eat-dog world in Monster Jam, especially when these two massive mutts make their way to the Monster Jam Triple Threat Series. Since debuting on the Monster Jam circuit, SCOOBY-DOO! has wowed audiences—especially when athlete Brianna Mahon revs up her Speedster. But Monster Mutt Dalmatian isn't one to be pushed out as new favorite Cynthia Gauthier's skills in all three styles of driving won't let up until her dog has had its day.

## Grave Digger vs. Zombie

It's a battle for the underworld, when two of the most fearsome competitors go head-to-head. Best to stay out of the way when the undead meets Grave Digger in the Monster Jam Triple Threat Series—both teams are out for blood (well, more like brains for Zombie).

# The Best of the World Finals

**World Finals I** The very first event in 2000 births the modern Monster Jam era with a freestyle competition full of high-flying athletic spectacle. Dennis Anderson and Tom Meents place at the top of the sport.

**World Finals VII** Grave Digger and Max-D clash in early racing rounds before splitting the two top championship prizes, cementing their rivalry.

| **2000** | 2001 | 2002 | **2003** | 2004 | 2005 | **2006** | 2007 | 2008 | 2009 |

**World Finals IV** El Toro Loco makes its Finals debut with an epic freestyle run in which athlete Lupe Soza lands the truck atop a semitrailer and leaves it for other athletes to navigate around. Talk about crazy!

When every car has been crushed and every jump has been landed across the Monster Jam season, it all comes down to the biggest jam of them all. Every March, the top thirty-two Monster Jam trucks of the year head to Las Vegas to compete for World Finals championship supremacy. And over almost two decades of competition, this event has provided some of the biggest moments in the history of the sport.

**World Finals XVIII** It was a great year for firsts in Monster Jam. Lee O'Donell landed the first front flip in VP Racing Fuels Mad Scientist, while the first ever reverse backflip AND the first forward momentum backflip were landed.

| 2010 | 2011 | 2012 | 2013 | 2014 | 2015 | 2016 | 2017 |

## World Finals XI

One for the books with the wild debut of multiple Grave Digger throwback models. The greatest ever racing final between Max-D and Grave Digger ends with Grave Digger rising up to victory.

**World Finals XVII** Returning to glory, Grave Digger completes its first ever Double Down championship by taking the top prize in both racing and freestyle.

# Going International

## The UK & Western Europe

It comes as no surprise that some of the most dedicated Monster Jam fans come from the motorsport communities of Europe. The very first international exhibition took place in Paris, France, in 2001, and since then Monster Jam has wowed crowds from Cardiff, Wales, to Frankfurt, Germany.

## Asia Pacific

Fans enamored with the major metal action of Monster Jam turned out big in 2016 for the sport's debut in Osaka, Japan. With Monster Jam legends Max-D and Grave Digger each winning in competition, attendees were given a week-long show they'll never forget.

## Central and South America

While Monster Jam travels south every year to entertain diehard fans in Mexico, recent years have seen the athletes and their trucks driving even farther. Cities like San Juan, Puerto Rico, and even Santiago, Chile, have welcomed Monster Jam with open arms, solidifying its global community ties.

## Australia

Perhaps no place on Earth outside North America is Monster Jam more appreciated than the land down under. For years, trucks like Team Hot Wheels Firestorm and Son-Uva Digger have toured across the continent, selling out stadiums in Brisbane, Melbourne, Adelaide, Sydney, and Perth.

# MONSTER JAM

## Achieves the IMPOSSIBLE

**A**t a moment's notice, you, the fan, could be plucked from the crowd of a Monster Jam competition to take part as an official Monster Jam judge! This six-person panel leads the way in scoring rounds, and Monster Jam is now putting the power of competition scoring in your hands. Listen to the host and watch the video screens so that you can be part of the Judges Zone right from your own seat!

But how can any one person judge a Monster Jam truck? What defines greatness when the average includes defying the laws of gravity or ripping apart the track?

In order to know Monster Jam fully, you have to learn the ins and outs of the unbelievable accomplishments these vehicles achieve daily. From physics-bending feats to jaw-dropping donuts, the following pages demystify the moves, jumps, and tricks that allow Monster Jam trucks to do the impossible.

2017
MONSTER JAM
XVIII
WORLD FINALS
Presented by
NGK
SPARK PLUGS
SAM BOYD STADIUM
RACING CHAMPION

# "Wow" Moments

The first rule of following Monster Jam freestyle is understanding that what looks like a daredevil stunt is actually a well-planned-out and practiced trick. Skilled athletes take their trucks right to the edge and cut it close to create these "wow" moments.

## Power Out

As a Monster Jam truck speeds and spins its way through a 120-second freestyle run without stopping, there's always the risk of a rollover, flipping the truck onto its roof. But the best athletes can kick out of this spiral with a well-timed burst of acceleration right when all hope seems lost.

## The Stoppie

The one thing you don't want to see after a competitor lands a major jump is a nose plant where the truck hits the dirt headfirst. Luckily, this

can be avoided with style thanks to the wow-inducing move called a stoppie or nose wheelie that tips the truck up on its front wheels.

## The Save

As old school as it gets, but still impressive, great Monster Jam athletes know how to take ultra-sharp turns and high-speed jumps to the limit without committing an endo or rolling the vehicle end over end. If you see a Monster Jam truck bounce back from such a move, recognize that you're in the presence of greatness.

## Crash-leticism

The biggest "wow" moments of all come when Monster Jam competitors don't just avoid damaging their own truck, but dish out some crushing too. Cars are placed all around the track for this very purpose. In fact, grinding up recycled autos is such a huge part of the Monster Jam legacy that the sport crunches up more than three thousand cars on the track each year!

# The Tricktionary

The acrobatic acts of Monster Jam trucks have blown up in recent years, so use this dictionary of the sport's greatest tricks to watch out for the most spectacular stunts.

The wow-worthy **WHEELIE** is a Monster Jam standard that still shows poise and patience on the part of an athlete. Athletes must be cautious and aware of their vehicle at all times, especially since flipping too far back has the potential to end their freestyle run!

One of the most famous automotive tricks in history is a stunt many ATV athletes are familiar with. But Monster Jam trucks pour on extra speed to create a dirt-spitting **DONUT** unlike any other to the wild cheers of fans.

Never to be outdone, most Monster Jam competitors look for action-oriented takes on classic moves. A favorite is the **SLAP WHEELIE**, which is when the truck pops up on its back tires after bouncing on its front end.

## SCIENCE JAM

Torque is a word for when a force rotates around an axis. For example, you use torque every time you turn a wrench or twist off a bottle cap. It's torque that allows a Monster Jam truck to stand tall when popping a wheelie.

The unstoppable **SKY WHEELIE** is even harder to achieve as the competitor has to hold a vertical position perfectly still.

For Monster Jam trucks with an eye on the rearview, the **REVERSE WHEELIE** is the way to go. This move involves zooming backward up a ramp for a blind jump before landing on your back wheels and holding that position.

In the modern era, nothing gets the crowd roaring like a **BACKFLIP**. While this midair reversal may seem standard today, it's still one of the hardest tricks to pull off. Yet athletes like Scott Buetow below are pushing the move ever forward by working to perfect backflips across the Monster Jam tours.

First credited to Northern Nightmare, the variation on the backflip called the **CORKSCREW** sees a Monster Jam truck turn side to side in the air rather than front to back, landing safely in the opposite direction from its liftoff to fan amazement.

No matter what twists and tricks Monster Jam trucks deliver next, there's nothing quite like seeing a competitor grab **BIG AIR**. The act of jumping over thirty feet high remains an all-time showstopper. And that's just the tip of a very big iceberg . . .

# The Long Game

**T**he longest jumps ever taken by Monster Jam trucks measure 130 feet, which is a distance longer than you might imagine!

At 130 feet, major Monster Jam jumps are as long as eighteen cars lined up side to side . . . or five adult giraffes . . . or one titanosaur—the longest dinosaur ever discovered!

# Freaky Physics

**A**ll the best Monster Jam athletes in the business have one thing in common: physics. They all know how to manipulate the laws of physics to get their craziest stunts off the ground. So just what is physics? Technically it's the science of matter and its motion through space and time. But for athletes, it's a gateway to the impossible.

## Out to Launch

Everything about how a Monster Jam truck completes a trick is based on force. The engine provides one force by spinning the wheels forward. When that spinning gets faster, we say the truck is accelerating. But another force affecting things is gravity. Gravity holds a heavy object like a Monster Jam truck firmly on the ground.

When a Monster Jam truck runs up a ramp, it can fight back against gravity for just a moment. But first, it needs to accelerate quickly enough to launch it into the air. The speed Monster Jam athletes have to hit to make this happen is at least forty miles per hour. In physics, this is called the launch velocity.

With the proper speed and a steep-enough ramp, Monster Jam trucks have been able to go twenty-five to thirty feet in the air. In 2016, daredevil athlete Tom Meents was even able to jump Max-D over six trucks!

# Spin City

When a Monster Jam truck spins a donut, it is because two forces are pushing on the body. The engine wants to push the truck forward. This is called inertia. However, when the athlete turns the wheels, it creates a competing force called centripetal force. Centripetal force is a circular force which causes the entire vehicle to spin toward its center. A similar thing happens when you take a bucket of water by the handle and swing it around in a circle with your arms extended. Try it. You won't get wet!

# Flipping Out

A backflip is even harder to achieve because Earth's gravity wants to pull the truck back down to Earth.

Whenever a truck speeds up a ramp, it gains momentum the more that force is applied to it. To make the backflip possible, the vehicle has to travel up a dirt ramp at a ninety-degree angle in order to create what is called angular momentum. This means it has to throw itself hard into a rotating pattern rather than simply push forward.

While many Monster Jam athletes have mastered the skill of shifting their momentum into the air for a backflip, Max-D and Meents are constantly working to push the trick even further. By completing two whole rotations in the air, the gravity-defying double backflip is achieved. But that stunt is almost impossible to land on the truck's tires because the unbalanced weight of the vehicle tilts the rotation quickly.

# Springing Forward

The most astonishing aerial trick in Monster Jam history involves such complicated physics that it's only been performed once: the epic forward flip!

Once again, Meents set out to challenge Max-D with a plan that would allow the truck to launch off a ramp and rotate in the air nose first. This stunt combines the launch velocity of a big-air jump and the angular momentum of a backflip, but it has gravity, weight, and balance working against its success.

To make an attempt, Team Max-D had to build a special Monster Jam truck body with a smaller wheelbase (for a better center of gravity) and additional coil shocks (to push the back tires forward). What's more, the ramp itself was a special "kicker ramp" with a catapult-like mechanism on its end. This gave Max-D one last push as it tried to rotate fully in the air before hitting the nose plant gravity had planned.

When Max-D finally tried the move live in 2015, it actually flipped twice! One rotation came in the air, and the other was a barrel roll that landed truck and athlete safely in the pages of history.

# MONSTER JAM

## PIT PARTY

**M**onster Jam fans celebrate their love like no other fandom on the planet—with the athletes and vehicles in person! Before select Monster Jam competitions, a fun-filled Pit Party is open to diehard fans featuring autograph sessions, barbeques, fashion competitions, and more. Whether you're at World Finals or your hometown arena, read on to see how you can fully embrace the Monster Jam lifestyle.

ARCHIE MANNING 71-82
Mercedes-Benz Superdome
Chevron
Ochsner
OFFICIAL MERCHANDISE
GRAVE DIGGER

# Meet and Greet

**M**onster Jam athletes love nothing more than meeting fans young and old in the Pit Party's many up-close autograph and photo sessions. Want to check your height against a massive tire on Max-D? Dying to show off your El Toro Loco Hot Wheels collection to the big bull's athlete? Wondering what tips your favorite athlete can share that will help you one day drive Grave Digger? It's all happening here, so come early and stay all day!

# Party Planning

**W**hether it's your first time or your five hundredth, getting ready to hit the Pit Party takes planning to get the full experience. Here are some signature Monster Jam events that will leave their mark on you, and after you're done, you may leave a little bit of yourself on the track.

## Track Walk

See the scope and shape of the Monster Jam event that you'll soon witness up close with this traditional parade of trucks and look at the major obstacles they're about to face. Think you've got the chops to take a 12,000-pound Monster Jam truck out on the tour? You won't know for sure until you see how big a Monster Jam competition really is from the athlete's perspective.

## Dalmatian Nation Fashion Show

When it comes to appreciating Monster Jam, fans don't just wear their hearts on their sleeves. They wear their pride in their favorite truck with wild hair, custom-sewn clothing, and matching everything in this beloved spotlight for everything Monster Jam. And at the annual World Finals, that means the Dalmatian Nation Fashion Show—an all-out style fest inspired by Monster Mutt Dalmatian! Come down to participate or just to cheer on the most creative fans in motor sports.

## Monster Jam Tailgate

Why not make it an all-day tailgate with a great All-American grill out? Enjoy the best burgers, hot dogs, and BBQ chicken and then double down for a second helping. You'll need the fuel it provides when you're jumping up and down during the freestyle event later.

What Monster Jam truck best speaks to your personality?
Take this simple quiz to find your one true fandom!

Are you a
**Night Owl?**

Do you hang out in
graveyards?

Are you an
**Animal Lover?**

Dogs or
livestock?

Are you a
**Wild Child?**

Are you a
musician?

| | | |
|---|---|---|
| **YES:** For thrills or for food? | Thrills | GRAVE DIGGER |
| | Food | ZOMBIE |
| **NO:** Do you want a boat or a tank? | Boat | Pirate's CURSE |
| | Tank | SOLDIER FORTUNE BLACK OPS |
| Show dogs or lap dogs? | Show | MONSTER MUTT DALMATIAN |
| | Lap | SCOOBY-DOO! |
| Livestock | | El TORO LOCO |
| **YES:** Punk rock or heavy metal? | Punk | MOHAWK WARRIOR |
| | Metal | DRAGON |
| **NO:** Do you build things or break things? | Build | EarthShaker |
| | Break | MAX-D MAXIMUM DESTRUCTION |

Part sport, part entertainment, pure adrenaline . . . **Monster Jam!**